THE COMPLETE PIANO F
JEROME KERN

Arranged by Kenneth Baker

Wise Publications
London/New York/Sydney

Exclusive Distributors:
Music Sales Limited
8/9 Frith Street,
London W1V 5TZ, England.

Music Sales Pty Limited
120 Rothschild Avenue,
Rosebery, NSW 2018,
Australia.

This book © Copyright 1990 by Wise Publications
Order No.AM80383
UK ISBN 0.7119.2349.3

Book designed by Pearce Marchbank Studio
Arranged by Kenneth Baker
Compiled by Peter Evans
Music processed by Musicprint

Music Sales' complete catalogue lists thousands of titles and is free from your local music shop, or direct from Music Sales
Limited. Please send £1.75 in stamps for postage to Music Sales Limited, 8/9 Frith Street, London W1V 5TZ.

Printed in the United Kingdom by
J.B. Offset Printers (Marks Tey) Limited, Marks Tey, Essex.

DEARLY BELOVED

Music by Jerome Kern
Words by Johnny Mercer

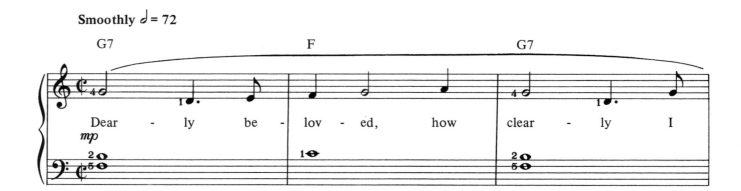

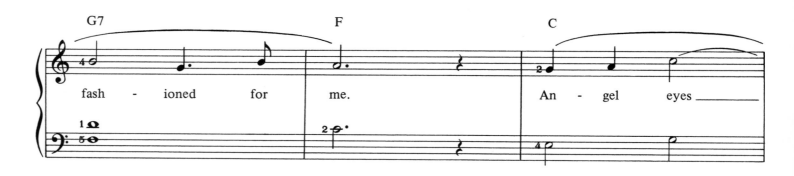

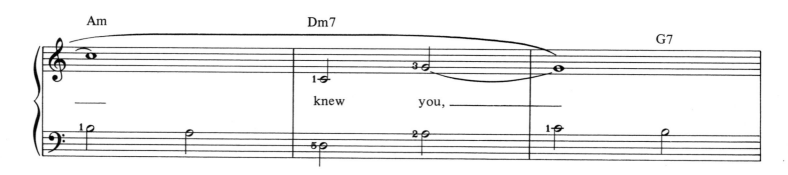

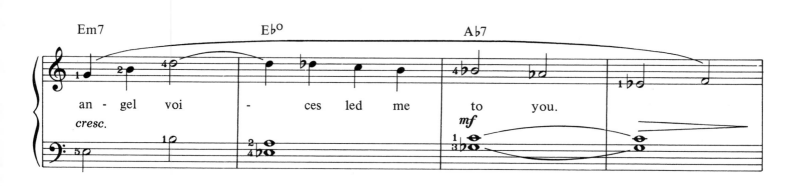

an - gel voi - ces led me to you.

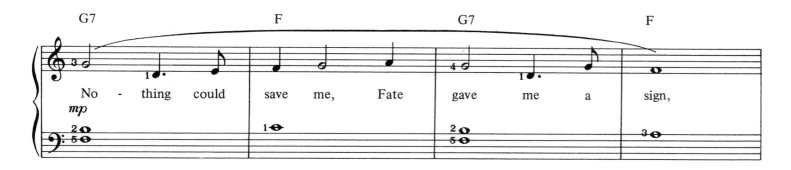

No - thing could save me, Fate gave me a sign,

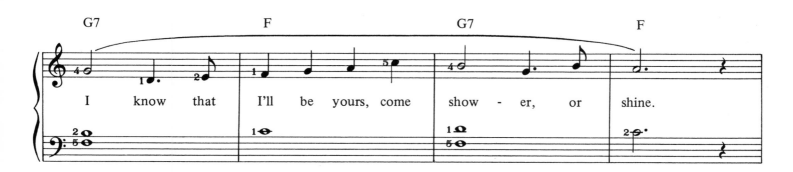

I know that I'll be yours, come show - er, or shine.

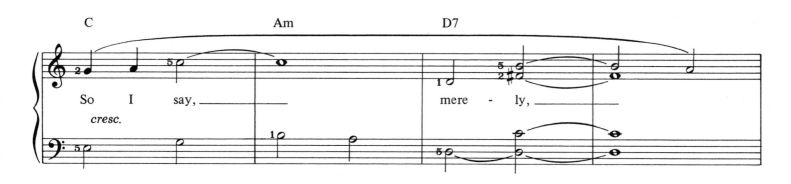

So I say, _____ mere - ly, _____

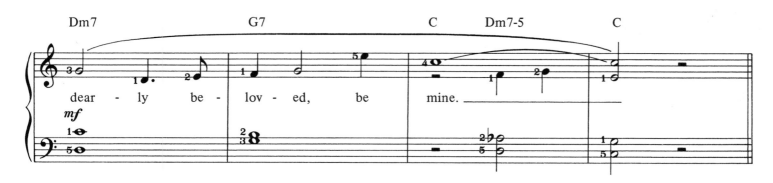

dear - ly be - lov - ed, be mine. _____

5

THE LAST TIME I SAW PARIS

Music by Jerome Kern
Words by Oscar Hammerstein II

With nostalgia ♩ = 69

The last time I saw Pa - ris, Her heart was warm and gay.
last time I saw Pa - ris, Her trees were dressed for Spring.

I heard the laugh - ter of Her heart, in
And lov - ers walked be - neath those trees, and

ev - 'ry street ca - fé. The
birds found songs to sing. I

1. The

2. I

dodged the same old tax - i - cabs that I had dodged for

CAN I FORGET YOU

Music by Jerome Kern
Words by Oscar Hammerstein II

A FINE ROMANCE

Music by Jerome Kern
Words by Dorothy Fields

THEY DIDN'T BELIEVE ME

Music by Jerome Kern
Words by Herbert Reynolds

I'M OLD FASHIONED

Music by Jerome Kern
Words by Johnny Mercer

CAN'T HELP SINGING

Music by Jerome Kern
Words by E.Y. Harburg

LONG AGO AND FAR AWAY

Music by Jerome Kern
Words by Ira Gershwin

MAKE BELIEVE

Music by Jerome Kern
Words by Oscar Hammerstein II

ALL THE THINGS YOU ARE

Music by Jerome Kern
Words by Oscar Hammerstein II

OL' MAN RIVER

Music by Jerome Kern
Words by Oscar Hammerstein II

I'VE TOLD EV'RY LITTLE STAR

Music by Jerome Kern
Words by Oscar Hammerstein II

SMOKE GETS IN YOUR EYES

Music by Jerome Kern
Words by Otto Harbach

PICK YOURSELF UP

Music by Jerome Kern
Words by Dorothy Fields

THE FOLKS WHO LIVE ON THE HILL

Music by Jerome Kern
Words by Oscar Hammerstein II

Our _____ ve-ran-da will com-mand a view of mea-dows green, _____ the sort of

view that seems to want to be seen. _____ And when the kids grow up and

⊕ CODA

what they have al-ways been called, _____

"The folks who live on the hill."

33

YESTERDAYS

Music by Jerome Kern
Words by Otto Harbach

CAN'T HELP LOVIN' DAT MAN

Music by Jerome Kern
Words by Oscar Hammerstein II

THE WAY YOU LOOK TONIGHT

Music by Jerome Kern
Words by Dorothy Fields

THE SONG IS YOU

Music by Jerome Kern
Words by Oscar Hammerstein II

BILL

Music by Jerome Kern
Words by P.G. Wodehouse & Oscar Hammerstein II

I WON'T DANCE

Music by Jerome Kern
Words by Oscar Hammerstein II & Dorothy Fields